Night

Macdonald

About Macdonald Starters

Macdonald Starters are vocabulary controlled information books for young children. More than ninety per cent of the words in the text will be in the reading vocabulary of the vast majority of young readers. Word and sentence length have also been carefully controlled.

Key new words associated with the topic of each book are repeated with picture explanations in the Starters dictionary at the end. The dictionary can also be used as an index for teaching children to look things up.

Teachers and experts have been consulted on the content and accuracy of the books.

A MACDONALD BOOK

© Macdonald & Co (Publishers) Ltd 1972

First published in
Great Britain in 1972

This edition first published in
Great Britain in 1986

British Library Cataloguing in Publication Data
Night. – (Starters)
    1. Readers – 1950 –
    I. Title
    428.6   PE1119
    ISBN 0-356-03999-4
    ISBN 0-356-11494-5 Pbk

Printed and bound in Great Britain by
Purnell & Sons (Book Production) Ltd,
Paulton, Bristol

Published by Macdonald & Co (Publishers) Ltd
Maxwell House
74 Worship Street
London EC2A 2EN

Members of BPCC plc

Illustrator: Janet Ahlberg

It is time for me to go to bed.
Soon it will be dark.

1

Most people sleep at night.
Many animals sleep at night too.

2

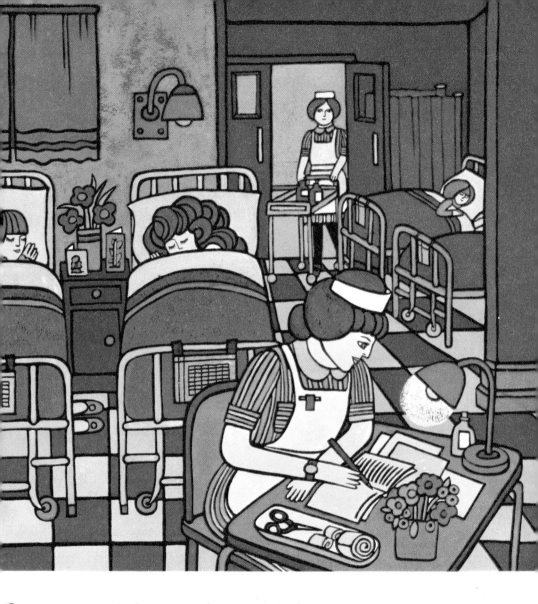

Some people work at night.
They sleep in the day time.
This nurse works at night.

3

This man is a nightwatchman.
He is looking after a factory.
He has not seen the robbers.

4

This machine prints newspapers.
These men work the machine at night.
People can buy the newspapers
in the morning.

Some people travel at night.
These people are sleeping
on a train.
They sleep while the train goes along.

Aeroplanes often fly at night.
People sleep in the seats.

Ships often sail all night.
They carry special lights.
Sailors on other ships see them.

The lighthouse stands on the rocks.
The lighthouse shows
where the rocks are.
Its light shines at night.

9

Night happens like this.
The sun shines on the world.
It shines on one side.
Where the sun is shining, it is day.
10

On the other side of the world,
it is night.

The world is always turning.
So night comes
to the places where it was day.

12

Night begins in the evening.
Night ends in the morning.

The moon shines at night.
People can see by moonlight.
14

Stars shine at night too.
They do not give much light.

cat

fox

badger

mouse

Many birds and animals
can see in the dark.

16

Owls hunt at night. They fly about
looking for little animals.
Owls can see well in the dark.

These animals are bats.
They fly at night.
Many bats eat insects.

18

In some countries
the bats are huge.
People call bats like these
flying foxes.

Many insects fly at night.
These moths are flying into the light.

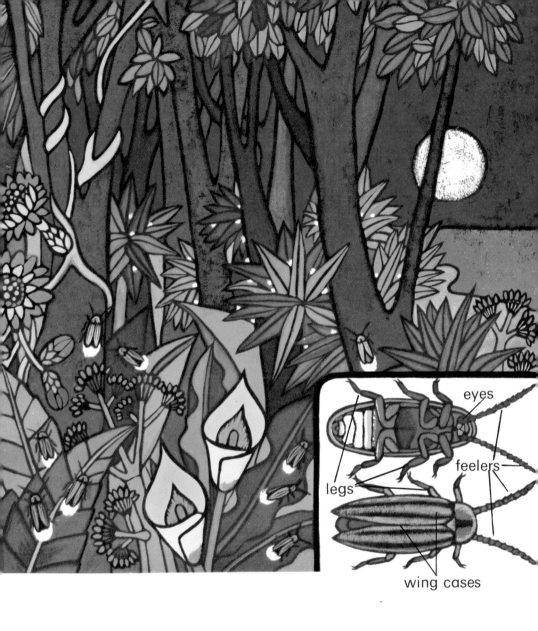

eyes

feelers

legs

wing cases

These insects are fireflies.
They can shine at night.

See for yourself

Make a model of the world.
Shine a torch on the model.
Pretend the torch is the sun.
You can see how day and night happen.

Starter's **Night** words

bed
(page 1)

factory
(page 4)

people
(page 2)

robber
(page 4)

animal
(page 2)

print
(page 5)

nightwatchman
(page 4)

newspaper
(page 5)

buy
(page 5)

ship
(page 8)

train
(page 6)

light
(page 8)

aeroplane
(page 7)

sailor
(page 8)

seat
(page 7)

lighthouse
(page 9)

rocks
(page 9)

bat
(page 18)

world
(page 10)

insect
(page 18)

stars
(page 15)

flying fox
(page 19)

owl
(page 17)

torch
(page 22)